fish·ing

fish·ing

an angler's dictionary

by Henry Beard
and Roy McKie

Workman Publishing · New York

Library of Congress Cataloging-in-Publication Data available.

ISBN-13: 978-0-7611-2642-3

Workman books are available at special discounts when purchased in bulk for premiums and sales promotions as well as for fund-raising or educational use. Special editions can also be created to specification. For details, contact the Special Sales Director at the address below.

Workman Publishing Company, Inc.
225 Varick Street
New York, NY 10014-4381
www.workman.com

Printed in the United States of America

First printing March 2002

10 9 8 7 6

To all those who have heard the call of the fish.

angler

angler One of two cold, wet, devious, and temperamental creatures of somewhat limited intelligence found at either end of a fishing line. See FISH.

angling

The art of fishing. The commonly accepted source of the term is the ancient Indo-European word *anka,* meaning "hook" or "fish with a hook," but several other words are more likely candidates, including *enka* ("foolish expenditure"), *unglo* ("one who is tormented by insects"), *onku* ("loud or frequent lamentation"), *angi* ("to deceive"), *inkla* ("to repeat a stupid act"), *onklo* ("possession by demons"), and *angla* ("love of suffering").

artificial Type of synthetic bait rejected by a finicky fish because it is too large or too small, has the wrong shape or coloration, or makes the wrong motion in the water. See NATURAL.

backing down

1. A maneuver in which the captain of a charter boat reverses his craft toward a hooked fish to remove stress on a fisherman's line. *2.* A maneuver in which the fisherman retracts ill-advised comments made to the captain following conversion of a prize fish into chowder in the boat's propellers. See CHARTER BOAT.

baffling

1. n. Compartmentalized interior construction of a down-filled sleeping bag. *2. adj.* Perplexing or puzzling, as in a *baffling* problem, like how to stuff a mass of portable bedding the size of a pony into a receptacle apparently designed to hold a shaving kit.

bait casting

Angling method whose key component is an open reel that must be carefully controlled by hand to prevent line-tangling backlash. Bait-casting gear is tricky to use, but many anglers prefer it because the sight of a jammed spool festooned with loops of knotted fishing line effectvely eliminates any interest fellow anglers might have in borrowing it and magically discourages requests for fishing advice or assistance.

bait casting

barbless hook

Hook from which the reverse-angle edge has been removed that is favored by masochistic anglers who want their fishing to be completely, rather than mostly, pointless. See HOOK and SPROAT.

barnacle

The only marine species of any size whose reported accumulation in significant numbers on a deep-sea fishing boat can be accepted without the need for independent verification. See PARTY BOAT and REEF FISH.

bass

By far the most popular freshwater game fish in the U.S. and Canada, offering an amazingly rich variety of sport. The fish may be of the smallmouth, largemouth, black, spotted, white, or yellow varieties; they may be fished on fly rods or spinning tackle, in lakes or rivers, wading or afloat, in spring or summer, with streamers, bugs, poppers, plugs, or flies; but despite this incredible angling diversity, all bass fishing has one thing in common: no bass has ever been caught in North America without at least one six-pack.

bend

1. The curved part of a fishhook. 2. The place anglers go around when the hook straightens out and a fish escapes. See HOOK and PLAYING.

billfish

Informal name for any large spear-jawed saltwater game fish, such as sailfish, swordfish, and marlin, which are so named because, following a day's outing in search of one of these magnificent creatures, the captain of a sport-fishing boat traditionally presents the angler who chartered her with an enormous bill in a short but often emotional dockside ceremony. See CHARTER BOAT.

blackfish

1. Common name for the tripletail and the tautog, two unrelated saltwater fish caught in coastal waters. 2. Common name for any fish caught in coastal waters frequented by oil tankers.

bluefish

Rapacious, carnivorous fish that, during feeding periods, will strike at almost anything, including other bluefish. The insatiable appetite of this popular game fish has made it an object of some disdain to sportsmen who prefer to test their skills against wilier and more elusive species. For these anglers, the challenge in bluefishing lies in finding something the fish will not bite. Snowflake paperweights, bicycle pumps, mood rings, yo-yos, and car parts have all been tried with varying degrees of nonsuccess, but it takes a special blend of inappropriate tackle and awkward movements of the rod to overcome a bluefish's hunger. It's a rare angler who doesn't come away from a stint in the surf or on a pier "full-handed," frustrated, and loaded down with "freezer ballast" as he disgustedly discards the old faucet, broken toilet tank mechanism, or other secret "sure loser" anti-lure he had placed his trust in.

bluefish

bluegill
1. Tasty panfish often sought by ice fishermen. *2.* Slang term for common condition usually suffered by ice fishermen. See PANFISH.

bluegill

bonefish

Skittish, much-sought-after game fish found in shallow-water "flats" in Florida, the Bahamas, and the Caribbean. Bonefishing can be a grueling and nerve-racking sport for the person working the rod, but it is exciting to watch and spectators often pause to take in the action as the angler goes through an amazing series of unpredictable movements, ranging from tooth-jarring slaps as a sand fly finds its target on a sunburned neck to breathtaking leaps when a piece of sharp coral pierces a shoe. And once in a while onlookers may be lucky enough to witness a sensational run when a small ground shark or poisonous manta ray sends the startled bonefisherman into a flurry of rapid strides and jerky hops as he churns the water white in a mad dash for dry land, filling the tropical air with a burst of unforgettably rich and colorful epithets.

book Handy package containing varying amounts of low-grade toilet paper for emergency use on long hikes through the deep woods, at remote campsites, or in poorly equipped lodges.

boot A shallow puddle worn on the foot. See PERCH, WADERS, WADING, and WATERPROOF.

branch
1. Tributary of a river or stream. *2.* Protruding limb of the only water-loving species found on a river or stream that an angler will claim to have hooked fewer of than he actually did and will never boast about the size of the largest specimen he ever caught.

branch

bug *1.* Large surface lure. *2.* Individual who is crazy about fishing. *3.* Insect that is crazy about *2.* See FLY BOX and INSECT REPELLENT.

bug

camera Small, relatively heavy receptacle employed by anglers to store small amounts of water and a canister of spoiled film. See PHOTOGRAPHY.

camp As used by anglers, a term denoting the place where the outboard motor broke and the cell phone ran out of power. See CHUB.

cane pole

The simplest fishing rig, consisting of a long stick with a length of line tied to its tip. A common bit of lore holds that a barefoot boy equipped with such a pole and using a plastic bobber as a float, a bent pin as a hook, and a worm as bait will go home with more fish than an expensively outfitted angler. Nonsense. There is no substitute for the subtlety of mind and singleness of purpose of the dedicated bait caster or fly fisherman. Possibly he flashes a bogus game warden's badge and confiscates the rascal's lucky catch; maybe he acquaints the lad with the horrors of reform school that await a truant who plays "fish hooky"; or perhaps he offers a "dough ball" of wadded money to the urchin, suggesting a few cavity-producing treats to take the place of a tiresome meal of trout. But whatever his methods, the experienced angler always gets the fish, for a youth's crude skill is no match for his cunning.

canoe Unique double-ended watercraft that provides comfortable seating for one and a half anglers with plenty of room left over for a foot or so of water. See PADDLE and PORTAGE.

carp
Prolific, long-lived, barely edible, nonnative nuisance fish whose only real value is its uncanny ability to mimic a fine bass or trout both in the course of its actual capture and—following its speedy return at high velocity to its nasty habitat—during imaginative retellings of the thrilling event to credulous fellow anglers.

casting
The art of propelling a lure toward a target using a forward, backward, sidearm, or underhand motion of the rod, depending on whether you want your fly, plug, or bait to end up in a tree in front of you, a tree behind you, a tree to the left or right of you, or a tree above you.

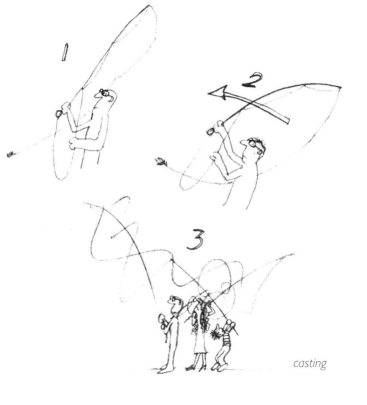

casting

catch-and-release

One of three increasingly common forms of no-kill fishing practiced by conservation-minded anglers. The other two, in which fish are never actually caught in the first place, are known as "lose-and-lie" and "nibble-and-fib." See RELEASE.

catfish

Although this weird-looking but very popular fish provides excellent sport for anglers, its primary value is as a commercial food product with huge fish-farming operations producing thousands of tons of firm, tasty, white meat annually for restaurants around the country where, depending on regional colloquialisms, it appears on menus as haddock, halibut, plaice, sole, sea bass, pompano, abalone, and veal.

char

1. n. Group of fishes, including the lake and brook trout, which are related both to salmon and to other trout.

2. v. Common method of cooking *1* over a campfire. See TROUT.

char

charter boat

Large, twin-engine oceangoing rented fishing boat fully equipped to take up to four saltwater anglers to the cleaners.

chicken

Popular non-seafood entrée sometimes referred to as "tuna of the land" often included on menus for individuals who absolutely refuse to eat fish, but who are for some reason happy with a bland form of poultry whose flavor is reliably reported to be indistinguishable from that of rattlesnakes, armadillos, lizards, alligators, turtles, frogs, monkeys, and bats.

chub

1. Informal name for the fallfish and various small carp. 2. Sound made by malfunctioning outboard motor during repeated attempts to start it. See KAPOK.

chum

1. Fishheads or innards, raw clams, smelly garbage, and the like, which are chopped up and thrown over the side of a boat to attract game fish. *2.* Dim-witted but friendly fellow angler who will chop up *1* and throw it over the side while you concentrate on keeping a recently eaten meal in its proper location.

club
Small wooden cudgel used to dispatch a fish by hitting it on the head, a far safer, quicker, and more humane method of putting it out of its misery than boring it to death with the story of how you caught it.

club

cod

Popular recreational fish and important commercial fish of the species *Gadus morhua* noted for a single large barbel on the tip of its chin, whose population has been depleted from its former incredible abundance to the point of near extinction by a land-dwelling mammal of the species *Homo sapiens* noted for a brain the size of a pea.

commercial fisherman

Individual who thinks that if you've got to wake up long before sunrise and travel for miles to get soaked, sunburned, seasick, cut, bruised, bug-bitten, and dog-tired trying to yank a bunch of slimy, angry animals out of the water, and then cut off their heads, scrape off their scales, and clean out all the gunk from their insides, you really ought to get paid for it. See GAME FISH.

crappie

Familiar name for a pair of closely related sunfish that allows an angler who is catching dozens of the tasty, sporty panfish to reply in all honesty to an unwelcome potential competitor who suddenly shows up rod in hand on the stream bank and inquires about the fishing, "oh, crappie, just crappie."

creel
Small, lightweight wicker basket or canvas bag in which freshly caught fish are placed to keep them cool and moist, typically with a capacity sufficient to hold around a dozen trout or bass, or to put it another way, a little more than 10 times the average angler's daily catch.

croaker, grouper & snapper

1. Informal names for three groups of popular saltwater game fish. 2. Informal names for the three types of unpopular anglers: the croakers who cough when silence is essential; the groupers who borrow your lures and help you lose fish during netting; and the snappers who respond to an angler's casual remark with a request that he go smoke a fish.

dam Elaborate, expensive, but extremely effective birth-control device installed on major rivers frequented by spawning salmon and steelhead trout. See LAKE.

darters

Small members of the perch family. The fight some years ago to save the Tennessee snail darter from extinction helped focus attention on these tiny, fast-moving fish, but for the dedicated group of fanatic anglers who pursue these little beauties throughout North America, darters have always had a value far out of proportion to their diminutive size. Armed with ultralight "pencil" rods, a few yards of 2-ounce line on a thimble reel, a barely visible "peewee midge" lure painstakingly tied to a dental floss leader, and a thumb net, these intrepid sportsmen stalk the shallow headwaters and creeks, waiting for the almost inaudible "pipple" of a "microlunker" darter breaking the surface and snatching the proffered bait in its minute jaws. Then, forefingers tensed to absorb the knuckle-wrenching shock of the sudden two- or three-foot darting maneuvers that give this plucky finned bantam its name, they play the colorful tab-tail for 10 or 20 seconds—it often seems more like a minute or two—until beached and quickly dispatched with a sharp flick of the fingernail, it joins the rest of the day's catch in the distinctive lapel creel that is the trademark of the darter enthusiast. A "keeper" in most states is ⅞ inch; 1½ inches or more is a very good fish; and anything over 3 inches is a fine trophy worthy of mounting on a tie clip or key chain.

darters

dawn Magical time of day when the only thing an angler has to do to absolutely guarantee that the fish will be biting like crazy is simply to stay home in bed. See DUSK.

dead water

Calm pools of water in large, slow-moving rivers or stagnant tidal areas where fish are rarely found and the only anglers present have Italian surnames and cement waders. See ESTUARY.

delivery

The use of a casting rod to airmail a lure to the wrong zip code. See FLY-FISHING.

dolphin
Aggressive tropical game fish that is not related to that playful, intelligent, and often helpful aquatic mammal, the porpoise. The confusion of the names is based on a superficial similarity in the shape of their snouts and not on any shared beneficial behavioral traits, as shipwrecked sailors have learned to their dismay when the dull-witted but malevolent dolphins push them off their rafts, eat their life preservers, and nudge them out to sea.

double-haul

Powerful but tricky-to-execute fly-casting technique that makes it possible to snag a lure in two trees at one time or higher up in a taller tree twice as far away. See FALSE CAST.

dusk Brief twilight period that separates the time when fish don't bite because they can see your line from the time when fish don't bite because they can't see your lure.

eel One of the very few fish you really wish had somehow gotten away. See SHARK.

estuary Technical term for a tidal transition zone where the pesticides, herbicides, and fertilizer runoffs that are killing all the freshwater fish upstream meet and mix with the ocean-borne oil spills, storm drain overflows, and medical waste that are poisoning all the coastal saltwater marine life.

false cast
Backward-and-forward whipping motion with a fly-casting line that usually results in a true test of patience, a genuine predicament, an honest-to-God mess, a veritable disaster, or a real pain in the ass.

false cast

fathom

1. n. Measurement of ocean depth, often made on fishing boats with an electronic sounding device called a fathometer. *2. v.* To comprehend, as in "I cannot *fathom* why I paid six hundred bucks for a useless metal box that shows that I'm in 5,000 feet of water when I'm tied up at the dock."

ferrule
Hardware fitting used to join together rod sections, consisting of a metal plug (male end) and a corresponding socket (female end) that are prone to a sudden, messy divorce during casts but invariably mate for life at the end of a long day of fishing.

fighting chair

Elaborate swivel-mounted seat in the stern of a deep-sea fishing boat in which a saltwater angler frantically pumping and reeling a hooked fish struggles with an overpowering urge to go to the bathroom.

filleting
Exciting but somewhat dangerous version of mumblety-peg played on a kitchen counter with a dull knife and a large fish. See GUT and SCALE.

fish
Remarkable aquatic animal typically weighing less than 10 pounds which, without gear, tackle, or equipment of any kind and using nothing more than hypnotic suggestion, can easily lure an angler as much as 50 times its size tens or even hundreds of miles into inhospitable terrain or unfamiliar waters and keep him there for hours with nothing more than a couple of false rises and a few practiced flicks of its tail. See PLAYING.

fishfinder

A bottom-fishing rig consisting of a sinker tied on a short length of line beneath a swivel holding a separate length of line with a baited hook on the end, also sometimes referred to as a rootfinder, a rockfinder, a tirefinder, a faultfinder, a weedkeeper, a temperloser, or a creekweeper.

fishing tip

Two or more pieces of contradictory angling knowledge or advice contained in a single phrase or sentence. See LORE.

fishing trip

Journey undertaken by one or more anglers to a place where no one can remember when the black flies arrived so early, the ice melted so late, or it rained so much.

flashlight

Handy device used to test the charge of batteries consisting of a metal or plastic tube with a small bulb at one end that indicates they are dead by failing to light.

flatfish

1. Any of a number of species of saltwater bottom fish characterized by a horizontal swimming posture. 2. Any fish left in the path of a beach buggy.

float fishing

Leisurely method of angling along a whole stretch of a river or stream in which the boat hits just about everything and the fish hit practically nothing. See STILL FISHING.

fluke

1. Summer flounder. *2.* Catching a summer flounder. See PARTY BOAT and REEF FISH.

fly Very light, artificial fly-fishing lure, of which there are two distinct types: the dry fly, which isn't supposed to suddenly sink the way it just did; and the wet fly, which shouldn't be floating up there on the surface like that. See PATTERN.

fly book Flat, portable leather or vinyl container holding a variety of supposedly reliable, time-tested, foolproof artificial flies, usually found in the fiction section of bait-and-tackle shops.

fly box

1. n. Plastic or metal container with separate compartments used to securely store and safely transport flies. *2. v.* To exchange blows in a sparring contest with any of the two-winged insects of the order Diptera. Anglers are generally not belligerent individuals, but it's common to see them engaged in furious bouts with a huge fly, bobbing and weaving and making quick jabs and thrusts at what seems to be thin air. Shrewd onlookers invariably put their money on the wily insect, favoring its agility, speed, and staying power over the angler's size, weight, and ability to absorb punishment (much of it self-inflicted), and these aerial featherweights seldom disappoint their backers.

fly-fishing

The most elegant, but also the most demanding form of freshwater angling. Unlike other methods of catching fish, in which the weight of the bait or lure provides momentum for the cast, in fly-fishing it is the line itself that is propelled toward the target, and 30 or more feet of this shooting line must be stripped off the reel and set into controlled motion overhead with precise, whiplike movements of the rod. Accurate fly-casting is very difficult to master, but it appeals to the angler who prefers finesse to force and measures success as much by the quality of the cast as by the quantity of the catch. Such a fisherman, standing in a crystal mountain stream, is the very epitome of grace and poise as he carefully gauges the wind and water and instinctively makes dozens of minor but crucial calculations. He moves the supple rod back and forth in an easy rhythm, and the faintly whispering line describes subtle parabolas in the air, the infinitesimal fly dancing at its tip, the hook sparkling in the sun. At last, with a final overhead stroke, he shoots the delicate loops through the air. Time stands still. And then a weird, almost animal cry shatters the silence as a well-honed barb bites into the posterior of an angler just downstream. Now comes the elemental test of a fly fisherman's mettle. Without a moment's hesitation, he cuts his line, nimbly makes his way to the stream bank, scoops up his gear, and deposits it in his car with a practiced flip of the wrist. Then, with deft hand motions perfected by long practice, he starts the engine, spins the wheel, and speeds away. Is he disappointed? No, for he'll soon fish again—in another county— and he has the satisfaction of knowing that, in a fellow angler's story, he's the one that got away.

flying fish

1. Remarkable tropical fish capable of skimming over the waves for 100 feet or more on tiny winglike fins. *2.* Any undesirable freshwater or saltwater fish, such as carp or scup, which, after being caught by an angler who thought he had hooked a trout or a striped bass, is propelled forcefully through the air with a brisk arm movement.

flying fish

fly tying
The art of attaching feathers, fur, wool, and silk to a tiny hook to create artificial lures that imitate insects, a skill easily mastered by anyone who can peel a grape blindfolded with a pair of tweezers and a butter knife while wearing oven mitts.
See PATTERN and TERRESTRIAL.

fork The point at which an unproductive river divides into two unpromising streams. See RIVER and STREAM.

gadget

Bright, alluring object with a sizable price tag placed in a prominent position in a bait-and-tackle shop right under the nose of a browsing angler.

game fish

Any fish sought primarily or exclusively for sport rather than for food or profit, which wise anglers choose to pursue in the knowledge that if they suffer a long dry spell, they will merely go crazy and will not have the additional unsettling experience of going hungry or going broke.

gear Anything you really wonder why you bothered to bring, or whatever would have come in very handy if you hadn't left it at home.

graphite

Remarkably versatile space-age material that makes it possible to manufacture fishing rods that are far too short but still have too fast an action, or too long yet much too slow.

gravel bar

1. Mound or bank of pebbles found in streams and rivers. 2. Candy product that has melted and resolidified in the bottom of a pack, tackle box, or duffel bag.

grip

The placement of the hand on the cork handle at the end of a rod, properly achieved by grasping it as if "shaking hands" with the rod and then holding it firmly until it is snatched out of the fingers by a sudden fish strike or an overeager cast, at which point the palm should be held straight out with fingers extended and moved from side to side to "wave it good-bye."

guide

1. One of a series of ring-shaped metal loops through which the line passes on a fishing rod. Typically, there is one just above the butt, several along the midsection, and one at the tip. *2.* Professional fishing assistant who in the course of planning the loading of a boat, the amount and type of provisions, and the degree of service to offer divides the angler into three basic sections: the butt, the midsection, and the tip.

gut To simultaneously empty both the contents of the stomach of a fish and the stomach of the squeamish angler performing the task. See SCALE.

habitat
Place about two miles upstream of where you are, on the other side of the river, near the No Trespassing sign, where a particular species of fish lives.
See RIVER and STREAM.

haddock

Important commercial ocean fish related to cod favored by preparers of institutional food since its firm flesh can easily be formed into sticks, cakes, lumps, slabs, nuggets, and balls, and generally will not disintegrate when cooked if coated with a protective batter made of equal parts plaster of Paris and blackboard chalk and fried for no longer than three hours at 1,100 degrees.

hat Anything on the head of an angler that does not bite or fly away when struck sharply with the palm of the hand. See VEST.

SOUTHERN NORTHERN WESTERN

NIGHT ICE PARTY BOAT

DRY FLY WET FLY SPORT

hat

hatch

Simultaneous appearance on a single stretch of stream of a large number of insects, such as the caddisfly, the mayfly, and the stonefly, which causes fish to rise and feed voraciously, making them somewhat susceptible to capture. It's impossible to predict the occurrence of a hatch, but your best bet is probably the day before yesterday.

hook

Irritating but highly reliable device used to quickly and precisely locate the position of one's thumb at the bottom of a tackle box. See LINE, SINKER, and SPROAT.

hot spot

1. Place on a given stream or lake, usually known only to locals, where fish can be found. 2. Place in the center of the palm of the right hand of a local where money may be placed to help find *1.*

hot spot

ice fishing

Winter fishing method in which anglers use a variety of specialized jigging or tip-up fishing gear to catch colds.

ice fishing

inchworm Small green

worm, the larval stage of several hundred species of moth, that is favored as food by trout and as bait by anglers, who, from force of habit, often refer to them as 6-inch worms, 10-inch worms, or foot-and-a-half worms.

indoor casting

Anglers anxious to improve their casting skills can profitably practice indoors. This is an ideal exercise, since it does away with the major inconveniences of fishing, such as cold water, bugs, tedious and costly trips to remote places, and the troublesome and messy fish itself, while preserving the display of delicate skill that is the essence of fine fishing technique. Seated by the pool with a cool drink or reclining on a comfortable "casting couch" in his own living room, the home angler can employ simple tackle and subtle casts to turn on a light, snatch a detective novel off a distant shelf, procure a snack from the kitchen, or restrain an unruly child. And for those who miss the realism of stalking a quarry, the appropriate gear may be used to have a little sport with the postman or the meter reader, obtain produce from a neighbor's garden, or walk a pet in bad weather without leaving the house.

indoor casting

in-flight testing

As a free service to anglers embarking on fishing trips, major airlines subject fishing rods, tackle boxes, and other gear to a series of rigorous trials intended to spot any flaws in design or packaging. There is no need to make special arrangements for this procedure; just hand over your angling paraphernalia at the check-in counter, where it will be immediately placed on a high-speed conveyor belt to begin its carefully planned ordeal. The exact testing process is a closely guarded industry secret, but based on an examination of fishing outfits that have undergone this shakedown, it involves the application of every form of compression, concussion, vibration, and perforation known to science, and if your rig emerges in usable condition at your destination, you can take justifiable pride in the knowledge that you are the owner of absolutely indestructible fishing equipment. See ROD CASE.

insect repellent

One of a number of "gag" items available in the novelty sections of tackle shops, along with "waterproof" clothing, "damp-proof" matches, and "long-life" batteries.

jackknife

Indispensable cutting tool generally found in the pocket of a different jacket, beneath the front seat of the car, or under the roll of screening on the table in the garage.

jig

Crude but effective artificial fishing lure made of a metal head and some form of dressing, designed to attract attention by its motion through the water rather than its resemblance to any particular food. Jigs are the simplest and most ancient of fishing lures, and in fact the oldest known evidence of angling is a carved elkhorn jig found deeply embedded in the bark of a petrified tree trunk unearthed in an exceptionally well-preserved

14,000-year-old Swiss lake village. Nearby were the sharply broken remains of a wooden pole, 70 feet of tightly tangled sheep's gut line, and a small leather pouch that held the skeleton of a single 2-inch-long lake minnow. See SPINNER and SPOON.

johnboat

Small, flat-bottomed, square-nosed craft so named because after a day of fishing it needs to be repeatedly flushed.

kapok *1.* Silky fibers used as stuffing in boat cushions. *2.* Promising backfiring sound made by outboard motor after 30 pulls of the starter cord. See MUMMICHOG.

keeper Any fish larger than the lure or bait used to catch it. See MEASUREMENT OF FISH, TROPHY, and UNDERSIZED.

keeper

knot

A tangle with a name.
See LEADER, SNELL, and
TAG END.

STEP I

STEP II

STEP III

STEP IV

knot

lake

Ecologists classify lakes as being oligotrophic (low in nourishment) or eutrophic (high in nourishment), and while terms such as these are of some interest to anglers eager to learn about the habitats and life cycles of various fish species, most fishermen prefer to know whether a given lake is autocatastrophic (approachable only by deeply rutted dirt roads); peptobismolic (unfit to drink from); psychomotorphobic (frequented by maniacs in overpowered speedboats); ectoplasmospasmodic (cold enough to cause extremities to freeze); or photosoporific (characterized by natural scenic beauty that leads fellow anglers to take hundreds of pictures of it for stupefyingly dull home videos). See PAY LAKE.

lateral line

Unique sensory organ found on the sides of fish that permits them to detect even the slightest vibration from far away, giving them plenty of time to vanish. Because of this faculty, fish can become aware of the approach of an unwary angler long before he casts his line simply by picking up all his careless little sounds, like the thud of a boot on gravel along the riverbank, the clunk of a trunk lid closing after the car was

parked, the scrape of tires on gravel
along the last mile of rough track,
the honk of a horn as a slow-moving
moron was passed back on the
highway, the clunk of the nozzle in
the tank during a stop for gas out
on the Interstate, the rattle of an
automatic garage door opening, the
sizzle of bacon being fried for breakfast,
the jangle of the alarm clock, and the
deep rumble of heavy snoring.

leader
Short length of light nylon monofilament or wire that connects the point where the knot at the end of the line slipped off to the place where the lure used to be.

leash Collective term for three fish, e.g., "a leash of perch." Two fish are a "brace," one fish is a "lot," no fish is a "bust" or a "bummer," and four or more fish are a "bunch," a "ton," or a "miracle."

license Permit issued upon payment of a modest fee that allows fishermen to lose lures in a specified area. See LIMIT.

lie

1. A place in a stream, river, or lake where fish lurk. *2.* Any simple declarative statement made by an angler about the location of such a place, or the number, size, and type of fish observed there, or the circumstances under which one or more of them eluded capture.

limit
Maximum number of a particular fish that an angler can take in a day. This number varies from place to place and species to species, but like the speed of light it is always so out of proportion to ordinary experience that it serves as a largely theoretical restriction with little practical application.

limit

line
Length of long, thin, strong synthetic material stretched between two fishing rods and joined at its midpoint by a pair of linked hooks. See SINKER.

line

live bait Something

slimy, smelly, or sickening
put on a hook to attract
fish, as opposed to
something shiny, sharp,
silly, or stupid.

lore
A fundamental misconception about catching fish couched in elegant language or conveyed in a simple, easily remembered piece of misinformation.

luck The only reasonable explanation for the fact that another angler caught all the fish in spite of your far superior skill.

lure Anything used to attract fish. There are basically two kinds of lures: those that anglers swear by and those they swear at.

maintenance

It only takes a few moments at the end of each fishing season to ensure that your gear will be in proper condition for use the following year. Of course, individual fishermen have their own maintenance programs, but they should certainly include the basic procedures listed here, which have been perfected over many years by countless anglers:

a) Dump reels into an empty ice chest—do not remove line.

b) Disassemble fishing rod and lean in closet corner next to umbrellas.

c) Place hat and leftover sunscreen in net and wedge behind washing machine.

d) Roll waders and vest into tight ball and toss down basement stairs.

e) Drop loose hooks and lures into creel and store in corner of garage.

f) Throw tools, gadgets, and knives into tackle box and put on a high shelf.

g) Freeze leftover bait in unmarked Ziploc bag.

map Handy schematic representation of all the various roads in the area which, unlike the one you are now on or are currently looking for, are large enough to be shown on a map.

matching the hatch

1. The practice of creating fly-casting lures that mimic the various stages of the life cycle of insect species favored by trout, from the time the flies hatch from eggs, shed their skin, swim to the surface, unfold wings and fly, until they ultimately mate and fall lifeless onto the water. *2.* The process through which an angler performs a similar metamorphosis as he fishes for trout, first emerging from his sleeping bag at dawn and briefly feeding voraciously, then, after embarking on a boat on the stream surface, suddenly rising unsteadily to his feet, extending his rod and casting, and finally moving into a brief but spectacular flying phase, followed by a longer aquatic or swimming stage.

matching the hatch

measurement of fish

The most commonly accepted parameters used in determining the length of a fish are: the distance from the center of the tail of the fish, while hooked, to the tip of the fishing rod; or from the snout to the end of the handle of the landing net; or from the gills of a fish held in the hand to the angler's elbow if he holds it horizontally or his foot if he suspends it vertically.

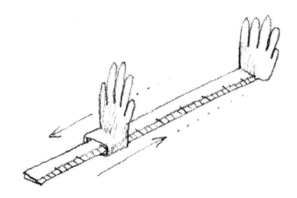

measurement of fish

mermaid
Legendary marine creature with the upper body of a woman and the lower body of a fish who should properly be referred to by more politically correct terms like merperson, aqua-American, terrestrially challenged individual, mythical-American, or differently real individual of interspeciated descent.

minnow Common term

for any small baitfish used to catch another larger fish, which can then be used in turn to catch a still larger fish, and so on, but even the most die-hard sportsman will at some point "cash in his fish" and "pocket the catch," and extra-prudent anglers can limit their risk from the very outset if they "take the minnow and run."

mummichog

1. Popular baitfish also known as killifish.

2. Disappointing sound made by the outboard motor on the 31st through 500th attempt to start it.

muskellunge

Extremely unpredictable and difficult-to-catch game fish in the pike family whose name comes either from the Ojibwa word for "mosquito bite" or an Algonquian phrase that translates roughly as "Hello, sucker."

myth Technical term for a basic piece of factual angling information contained in any given fishing book when referred to by the author of another fishing book.

natural Type of organic bait rejected by a finicky fish because it is the wrong size, the wrong shape, the wrong color, or makes the wrong motions in the water.

net

1. Woven mesh bag attached to a circular frame mounted on a handle that looks a little like a very loosely strung tennis racket, used by anglers to land or boat a hooked fish, often with a weak forehand or backhand scooping motion that goes way wide of the line or catches the top of the net, leading to a break point that gives the fish a chance to stay alive.

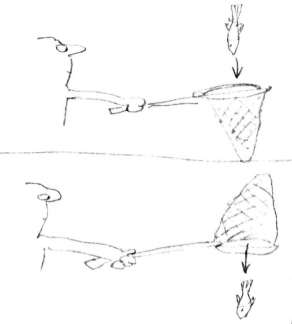

net

night crawler

Familiar term for the common earthworm, one of the most popular and consistently effective types of bait, whose uncanny ability to lure a creature that almost never encounters one in its natural habitat casts considerable doubt on the concept of fish as "brain food."

nymph

1. The underwater stage of certain insects eaten by fish or any wet fly pattern designed to imitate it. 2. The words "net!," "now!," "no!," "nuts!," or "ninny!" as spoken to a companion by a fly fisherman holding loops of shooting line in his mouth.

oar Heavy, long-handled wooden boat implement used to scare away pesky fish. See PADDLE.

Ob Siberian river familiar to anglers who have spent a rainy day in a cabin with a 47-card poker deck, the March 1987 issue of *Field & Stream,* and 20 filled-in crossword puzzle books.

opening day

The first day of the angling season in many parts of the country is April 1, which is often referred to by the name April Fisherman's Day or a similar term honoring anglers, and even nonfishermen get into the spirit of this popular national pastime by practicing harmless deceptions on one another.

opening day

ouananiche

French name for the wily and skittish landlocked Quebec salmon, which is also referred to by local French-Canadian fishing guides with earthier terms, like "sacrebleufish," "fichepecheur," "bête de la rivière," "cassecouilles," "emmerdeur," or "poissonofabiche."

paddle

Short, flat-bladed handheld oar used to keep the occupants of a canoe moist. See PORTAGE.

panfish

Anything removed from the water that will fit into a frying pan and does not melt, smolder, give off sparks, or explode when cooked.

party boat

Large saltwater fishing craft that carries a number of anglers, each of whom is charged a fee for the outing, which usually covers bait and the use of fishing tackle. Party boats are often crowded, and since the individual who catches the largest fish of the trip wins a pool of money made up of contributions by all on board, tempers can flare in close quarters when lines become tangled or a hooked fish is lost. For this reason, abiding by some simple shipboard etiquette is vital: a fellow angler should always be tapped lightly on the shoulder from behind before being punched on the nose or chin; if bait has been handled, hands should be washed before being placed around the neck of another fisherman; anyone who fails to respond to a slow ten-count is presumed to have given up his position at the rail; and no one should ever be thrown overboard while the fish are biting.

party boat

pattern

Characteristic size, shape, color, and texture of a fly-fishing lure. Although there are hundreds of patterns, most fall into one of two categories: "dummies" or "foolers," with a proven ability to alarm and annoy fish, that are prominently displayed on a hat brim or vest pocket and generously lent to fellow anglers; and "actuals," highly effective stream-tested designs that are hidden in a fly book or tucked away in an inside pocket.

WET BLANKET

GIBB'S DUD

FLASH IN THE PAN

CLOUSER'S TURKEY

DAVE'S DUFFER

COMPARADUNCE

GRIFFITH'S GOOF

GOLD-RIBBED PIG'S EAR

WULLF'S BANE

WOOLLY DOOFUS

pattern

pay lake
A fishpond or similar small impoundment stocked with easily caught hatchery trout or panfish where anglers are charged a fee to fish. Most of these enterprises are honest, but *caveat piscator:* there are a number of "bait-and-switch" operations that offer exciting but rigged diversions like "three-carp monte" and "crappie shooting," and unwary anglers can end up going home with both empty pockets and empty creels.

perch

1. Popular panfish found in a number of habitats. *2.* Standing place, such as a slippery bank, wet rock, or rickety dock, from which an angler was fishing for perch shortly before he unexpectedly entered his prey's habitat.

pet fish

1. Small fish, typically goldfish or colorful tropical species, kept in an aquarium or fish tank as a hobby. 2. Notoriously unsuccessful toy introduced during the Pet Rock craze by the ill-starred SnaFoo company, manufacturers of the Tango Hoop, the Busbee Flying Derby, and the Spittle Ball.

pet fish

photography

Ideal method of recording for posterity the capture of a prize fish. Anglers who hesitate to take snapshots of an unimpressive catch because of an obsolete belief that cameras cannot be made to lie should consider purchasing one of the new Scamcam digital models with a hyperbolic autofocuspocus lens and any of the excellent computer graphics photomanipulation programs like Photo Doctor, PictureThis, or FilmFlam.

pickerel & pike

Family of rapacious, malevolent, razor-toothed freshwater game fish that will strike instantly and violently at just about any lure you decide not to try.

plastic lures

Lifelike and effective plastic imitations of worms, frogs, squid, and other favorite foods of fish are widely employed by anglers, but even savvy sportsmen are unaware of some other equally convincing and useful streamside accessories, including the incredibly realistic 12-foot Vinylmouth snake which, when placed in a highly visible spot, can reliably clear a mile or two of stream of competing anglers in less than a minute, and the radio-controlled Mesmerizers, a pair of totally believable motorized rubber decoys of either a 14-inch rainbow trout or a 22-inch largemouth bass that are capable of executing several dozen preprogrammed teasing maneuvers designed to keep potentially bothersome fellow fishermen glued to a worthless downstream pool or a barren stretch of lakeshore for hours on end.

playing

1. Series of pumping and reeling motions used by the angler to tire a hooked fish and eventually drive it, in a state of exhaustion, into a net. 2. Series of nibbling motions, tail flips, and jumps used by a fish to madden a hooked angler and eventually drive him into a state of mind that will result in someone coming after him with a net.

playing

plug

Large, chunky plastic or wooden lure with treble hooks that is designed to imitate the sound and movement of baitfish as much as their appearance and to provoke strikes by creating a commotion rather than through clever camouflage. Divers, poppers, wobblers, and chuggers have long been popular but recent years have seen an explosion of new types, like the miniature underwater radio-powered lures, the rappers and hip-hoppers, that drive fish crazy with their irritating beat; the beepers, which produce a series of annoying electronic tweets; the solicitors, which make a ringing sound during evening feeding times, followed by a weird, burbling spiel; and the robbers, which sound exactly like a car alarm.

poaching

1. Stealing fish. *2.* Method of disposing of the evidence by boiling or steaming it into an unrecognizable bony sludge.

pocket water

1. Stream surface condition characterized by pools of water that form downstream from large rocks. *2.* Small impoundment of water often encountered by anglers when fishing for keys, change, folded money, or matches.

poncho

Portable sweat hut, steam room, and sauna. See TENT, WADERS, and WATERPROOF.

portage

The shortest distance between two hernias. See CAMP, CANOE, and FISHING TRIP.

presentation

The art of using a precisely executed casting motion to propel the totally wrong lure with just the right force into the absolutely perfect spot on the water.

presentation

put down
To spook a fish. Although fish see things differently than humans do, most have good vision, and unfamiliar shapes can scare them off. Anglers eager to improve their chances of getting close to skittish species, like wild trout, have gone so far as to invest in modern dance lessons to be able to imitate saplings or shrubbery, but a simpler method is to acquire one of the new, amazingly realistic rubber fish suits with lifelike scales and swim-fin

waders. Another excellent choice if money is no object is the MotorMaggot, a natural-looking 14-foot mechanical caterpillar with comfortable fishing positions for two anglers whose rods project through apertures in the "head," mimicking an insect's antennae, and a unique muffling system for its powerful diesel engine that makes its exhaust noises resemble the sounds of a cicada or a June bug, albeit an unusually large specimen.

records

The world record catches of game fish are routinely published in periodicals devoted to fishing, but significant accomplishments in other angling categories are less widely celebrated:

TIRE: 1986, Lake Ontario, 46½ pounds, 34 inches in diameter.

BOOT: 1991, Boston Harbor, 7¼ pounds, size 11 wide.

METAL OBJECT: 1985, Colorado River, MammaMia pasta maker, 21 pounds, 34 inches to tip of power cord.

NONMETAL OBJECT: 1979, Santee Reservoir, Party Time Play Mate Beer cooler, 11 pounds.

ANGLER (OTHER): 1996, Beaverkill River, 247 pounds.

ANGLER (SELF): 2001, Montauk Point, 304 pounds.

reef fish
Any of a variety of bottom fish often taken from party boats or "head boats" in ocean waters. The most critical part of reef fishing occurs long before the fishing grounds are reached. This is the all-important "rise," which takes place in the dark about 5 A.M. when the dramatic "strike" of an alarm clock turns the motionless, quiescent angler into a thrashing, seething mass of elbows and bedclothes, and sends him into

a heart-stopping "leap." If at this point the clock is thrown sharply across the room with an abrupt, powerful arm stroke, then chances are that the angler is about to enter a prolonged dormant phase and the fishing is likely to be a real snoozer.

reel
Cylindrical device attached near the end of a fishing rod for winding up or letting out line. There are several different types, but they all offer the angler the same option of two basic settings: "wheeeeee," in which at the slightest pull the line is payed out in a series of erratic loops at very high speed; and "fonk," in which the reel suddenly stops revolving with a sharp metallic sound, instantly dividing the line into two sections of unequal length.

reel seat The place on the grip end of a fishing rod where the reel was located before it decided to get up and go for a little swim just as you hooked a fish.

release

To let a just-caught fish go after removing the hook from its mouth and, if necessary, reviving it by holding it briefly in the water with its head pointed upstream until its gills start moving and it swims away, or, if it fails to respond, by giving it a light dusting with blackened redfish seasoning powder and showing it a picture of Emeril Lagasse.

retrieve

Fly-fishing maneuver in which a fished-out cast is taken off the water with a snapping, rolling, or waving motion of the line known as the "pick-up," "screw-up," "foul-up," "louse-up," "hang-up," "blow-up," or "oh, shut up."

river
Any stretch of moving water large enough to be crossed by a bridge from which fishing is prohibited. See STREAM.

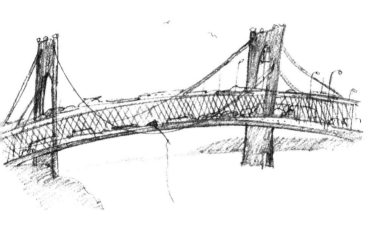

river

rod
Flexible, tapered stick that is the basic tool of angling. A rod of even medium length is awkward to carry, but anglers have found through long experience that it can be easily shortened with an ordinary car door, station wagon tailgate, or trunk lid.

rod case
Handy piece of rugged, impact-proof luggage that protects a fragile and expensive fishing rod, particularly during a long airplane trip to some continent other than the one where you were planning to fish.

rod casting

The discouraged angler who has decided to bid farewell to his hobby should do so with the same attention to form that he displayed when he practiced it. Stand on a stream bank, lake shore, pier, or beach and grasp the fishing rod by the cork handle. Select a sinker large enough to overcome the natural buoyancy of the rod, attach it securely to the line, then slip the hook over the lowest guide, tightening and locking the reel so that the rod has a slight bend. Hold the rod out straight in front of you, smoothly raise your arm over your head until it is almost parallel with the ground, and then, with a fast, overhead whipping motion of the arm, propel the rod forward. Just before release, give a quick snap of the wrist, and as the rod strikes the water, "dust" your hands with a few brisk sliding motions of one palm across the other, then raise your right hand and extend your middle finger.

rules of thumb

Given the considerable number of different fishing techniques, very few angling maxims have universal application, but the handful that do are worth remembering:

* It's probably a carp.
* It's not a good sign that the line got a lot lighter.
* That fish didn't jump because it was sad.
* It was definitely a trout.

* That branch isn't wiggling because the tree is trying to tell you something.
* Yanking on it won't do any good.
* It's deeper than it looks.
* There really is more water in the boat than there was five minutes ago.
* It is poison ivy.
* That was thunder.
* It's the wrong path.
* They're not in the other pocket.
* They're not in the tackle box.
* They're locked in the car.

sailfish
Large, highly prized saltwater game fish with a wide, distinctive, sail-like dorsal fin. Anglers, particularly nearsighted ones, should ensure that this sail is not imprinted with a number or logo, that the tail does not have a peculiar tiller-like appendage on it, and that there is no telltale "sailor" sitting on top of the "fish" before attempting to reel in a hooked specimen.

salmon

Magnificent freshwater and saltwater game fish related to trout. During the rare times when the salmon are running, they provide some of the most sensational sport in fishing, and during the long periods when they aren't, they still offer an incredible bounty of odd but useful words like kype, redd, parr, vomer, milt, smolt, grilse, and kelt for terminally bored anglers playing endless Scrabble games in backwoods cabins.

sardine

Term for a young herring, a commercially important fish typically packed in small flat cans as tightly as anglers on a party boat.

scale

To use a thin, curved knife to remove the overlapping bony ridges found on the outer skin of many fish and distribute them over the countertop, the sides of the cabinet doors, the floor, the walls, and the ceiling of a kitchen.

scales
Specialized measuring instrument used to determine the exact poundage of a potentially record-setting catch, like that fine saltwater game fish that ran amok after being boated and somehow managed to swallow a couple of dozen heavy sinkers, an 8-pound lantern battery, and four feet of anchor chain before being subdued and brought to the dock for a formal weigh-in.

scales

school

1. A large collection of fish of the same species like herring, mullet, alewives, or menhaden migrating or feeding together. *2.* A large collection of fish, like chumps, suckers, gudgeons, marks, boobs, greenhorns, or sapheads wasting money trying to learn fly casting together.

scrod *1. n.* Commercial fishery name for young cod or haddock fillets. *2. v.* Having had been unfairly dealt with in a business transaction at a sporting goods store or bait-and-tackle shop.

seafood

Anglers who live near the shore can be assured of a ready supply of delicious and healthful fish products with a minimum of trouble and expense if they keep their eyes open and use a little common sense. There's no need for costly rods and reels or budget-busting boat charters, because telephone companies in most areas have thoughtfully listed the likeliest spots where fish can be "taken" in a bulky but useful guidebook printed on yellow paper. You'll be in luck any time from about nine in the morning until early evening (except on Sunday), and the only "lure" you need to snag a basketful of yummy fillets or steaks (no need to clean these babies!) is the ever-reliable plastic "blade" with its distinctive magnetic strip or a little old-fashioned dough or bread, although if you insist on some sport, you can always try your luck with a rubber check.

seaweed
Form of marine life sought after by vegetarian anglers. With the exception of giant kelp, most species of algae don't put up much of a fight, but for the avid "musherman" on an oceangoing "scumboat" the deceptively offhand remark from a crewman that "it looks like there might be some algae up ahead," followed by the sodden gurgle as the large weeder hooks bite into the shimmering green or

brown mass and then the arm-numbing struggle to boat the bubbling glob of treacherous goo, is the stuff of oft-told tales whenever two or three "wortsmen" gather for a bowl of sea lettuce and some clam juice and swap stories of man against muck and "the ton that got away."

setting the hook

A small jerk used to drive the point of the hook into the mouth of a fish that just struck the bait cast by that considerably larger jerk fishing right next to you.

shad The only fish that is actually more difficult and time-consuming to eat than to catch.

shark
Large, exciting, but dangerous predatory saltwater fish that is the only living creature commonly found in coastal areas capable of being a consistent and serious threat to human life without ever getting behind the wheel of a powerboat.

shark

sinker A lead weight in any of a variety of shapes and sizes attached to lines or terminal tackle to facilitate the speedy disposal of unwanted lures.

skiff A slow leak surrounded by a relatively small, lightweight, boat-shaped piece of wood. See WADING.

smelt *1. n.* Small, oily fish that is found in large schools in both fresh and salt water. *2. v.* Discovered or located through the use of the olfactory sense, the most reliable method of finding a mislaid fish.

snell

Name of a knot used to attach the end of a leader to the shank of a hook without passing it through the eye. Other specialized knots used in fishing include the Nail Knot, the Clinch, the Blood Knot, the Perfection Loop, the Duncan Loop, and the Bimini Twist, but most anglers rely on a few old reliables, like the Hangnail, the Clump, the Sweat and Tears Knot, the Blooper, the Dunkin Don'tknot, the Knicker Twist, and the Fisherman's Noose.

sockeye

Familiar term for a species of landlocked dwarf salmon more properly called kokanee that is thought to be derived from an angler's typical response to disparaging comments made by a a fellow fisherman on the laughably small size of the specimen he caught.

solitude The state of being closer to nature than to the nearest flush toilet. See BOOK.

spearfishing

Unique underwater angling method that combines the sports of diving, fishing, and hunting, and, when sharks, barracuda, or manta rays are sighted, Olympic swimming.

spearfishing

special Term used to describe a custom-designed lure that fails to work on a particular species of fish at a specific location or under unique conditions as opposed to a lure that is generally useless.

spinner

Fishing lure consisting of a metal blade with a hole in it that spins or wobbles freely on a swivel. The most common shapes are the Indiana, the Colorado, and the Idaho, but many anglers prefer the Texas (a solid silver disk the size of a hubcap); the California (a bronze lotus leaf imprinted with a Tibetan mandala); the Connecticut (a tie clip); the Louisiana (an old license plate); and the New Jersey (a flat slab of lead designed to stun fish on the cast).

spinning gear

Inelegant and untraditional but extremely simple-to-use rod with a trouble-free, backlash-proof reel used by anglers who would rather fish for fish than fish for compliments. See TRADITIONAL and UNSPORTING.

spoon Type of metal fishing lure popular on backwoods fishing trips since if it is unsuccessful in attracting fish, it can at least be used to consume the contents of a can of Dinty Moore beef hash.

sproat Popular all-purpose hook with a parabolic curve. Other more specialized designs include the O'Shaugnessy, the Limerick, the Aberdeen, and the Eagle Claw, known more familiarly to anglers as the O'Shit, the Palmprick, the Stababun, and the Mangle Paw.

squid

Common name for members of the Cephalopoda family widely used as bait for saltwater game fish that is derived from the sound they make when dropped in a bucket or stepped on.

still fishing

Fishing technique usually characterized by a long stretch of time spent by an angler lying quietly, followed by a shorter period during which he lies noisily.

stream

A narrow watercourse small enough to be privately owned by someone who does not fish and hates fishermen.

strike
The thrilling moment when, with a quick rolling or lunging motion, an unseen finned quarry suddenly takes the hook of an angler fishing the spot you left five minutes ago.

striped bass

Widely favored, delicious, and beautiful game fish eagerly sought by commercial fishermen for profit and recreational fishermen for sport. Even though the commercial fishery is thought to account for well over two-thirds of the landings, surprisingly enough, seven out of every three striped bass reported caught last year were claimed by sport fishermen.

surf casting

Angling for shore-feeding fish, usually from a beach. Although the best fishing is generally in early morning and early evening hours, surf casters must be alert to the presence of swimmers— large, semiaquatic creatures who are normally quite playful but can become extremely ill-tempered when hooked.

surf casting

tackle
Any fishing gear which, when left on the ground, a pier, or the bottom of a boat, is capable of suddenly halting an angler's forward progress toward a desired goal.

tackle

tackle box

Portable plastic container that puts a wide selection of lures and hooks right at an angler's fingertips and, as he pokes through the various trays and compartments for a favorite plug or spinner, right into his fingertips.

tag end

The tail end of a fishing line that is looped, wrapped, turned, twisted, or laced around the standing portion of the line in a futile effort to reproduce a knot illustrated in a fishing book by an angler who is fit to be tied and will shortly come unraveled.

tarpon
For many saltwater anglers, the numerous outstanding qualities of this large, powerful, but primitive game fish make it the perfect quarry: it is found only in places that cost a fortune to get to; it is usually accompanied by sharks; it is very hard to hook and, once hooked, equally difficult to boat; when boated,

it usually has enough fight left to injure an angler and damage the boat; it has hundreds of large, sharp scales; and its flesh is bony and inedible. All it really lacks are poisonous spines or stingers and the teeth of a piranha, but presumably crossbreeding will one day correct these drawbacks.

tent Cumbersome device composed of fabric, tubing, ropes, and small metal stakes used by anglers camping in the woods to accumulate large amounts of water and collect specimens of local insects.

terrestrial
Term for a type of fly like the Muddler or the Hopper designed to imitate a ground-dwelling insect that fell in the water. Similar lures tied by an exceptionally clumsy angler that resemble insects that landed from another planet, like the Klingon Blood Worm, the Vulcan Earwig, or the Borg Drone Queen, are known as extraterrestrials.

test

1. A measure of the breaking point of fishing line, which can be anywhere from 2 pounds to more than 100. *2.* A trying or difficult fishing experience that reveals the breaking point of an angler, which can be anywhere from one or two lost fish in half an hour to zero fish caught in 10 days.

test

thermometer

Handy portable temperature-measuring device that lets an angler instantly determine whether the fish are not biting because the water is too cold or the fish are not biting because the water is too warm.

thumb One of five finger-like appendages of limited mobility found at the end of each of the hands of an angler attempting to tie a fly.

tippling

Method of fishing usually practiced around sundown in which each cast is followed by a short pull or tug on a hip flask. After several such "rod belts," casting can become erratic, but after a short period fish are caught two at a time.

tippling

traditional

Term used to describe any fishing technique that was conclusively proven to be impractical, ineffective, unnecessarily costly, or impossibly time-consuming prior to the year 1900. See UNSPORTING.

trash fish

Any species of fish that was once considered commercially undesirable but now, with fishing pressure growing on stocks of more valuable types, has been renamed and is actively marketed, including Grunge ("Summer Plaice"), Swinefish ("Sweetfish"), Gumhead ("Black Snapper"), Scumsucker ("Rock Fluke"), Ratfin ("Sea Pheasant"), Sludgeon ("Gray Trout"), Sea Scab ("Sugar Cod"), Stinker ("Green Sole"), and Skulkin ("Surf Bass").

treble hook

A wicked-looking compound hook with three separate barbs found on many plugs, spoons, and spinners that makes it possible to snag yourself and a fellow angler with the same lure that caught a fish.

AN ANGLER'S DICTIONARY | 259

trolling
Fishing method in which a baited line or lure is trailed through the water from the stern of a moving watercraft in the forlorn hope that its motions will be so enticing to a fish that it will somehow overlook the fact that there is a large boat on the other end.

trophy

Any fish that weighs
more than the gear
used to land it.

trophy

trout

Extremely sporty and truly delicious mostly freshwater game fish in the salmon family with several distinct varieties. The best known are the Brook (or Squaretail), the Brown, the Rainbow, the Cutthroat, the Lake, and the Golden, but most anglers encounter the shyer and more reticent subspecies like the Spooked (or Hightail), the Down, the No-Show, the Cut-Out, the Break-Off, and the Goldbrick.

tuna
Any of several valuable, hard-fighting saltwater fish in the mackerel family, including Albacore, Bigeye, Blackfin, Bluefin, and Yellowtail, that range in size from 8 to well over 1,000 pounds. Commercial and recreational fishermen alike dream of landing a sushi-quality Giant Bluefin worth $25,000 or more, but most catches have meat of a lower grade, like Seafood, Salad, Sandwich, Casserole, Loaf, Catfood, Fish Meal, and Sorry, Charlie.

undersized

A fish of a length too short or a weight too small to be legally kept. Anglers take note: a pair of undersized specimens caught in quick succession whose combined measurements meet the minimum does not constitute a "double-catch," a "family unit," a "joint effort," or a "twofer" even if both fish are of the same species and seem to know each other.

unsporting

Any fishing technique that has as its chief object the capture of fish rather than the accumulation of fishing equipment or the collection of angling memorabilia.

vest
Ideal utility garment for anglers. In its pockets, or clipped to its fabric on fixed or retractable lines, anglers carry a large number of tools, accessories, and gadgets which, while perhaps not absolutely essential, nevertheless make for more enjoyable angling. There are hundreds of gizmos and doodads to choose from, but certainly no fisherman should be without these basics: a padlock pick; a pair of wire cutters; a set of false-nose-mustache-

and-eyebrow glasses for a quick disguise
during embarrassing mishaps; a can
of pepper spray; a pocket dictionary
of epithets, either the classic *Blue
Streak Handbook* or *Hoffman's 1,001
Streamside Imprecations;* a small casette
recorder with tapes of wolf howls,
bear growls, and bobcat shrieks;
a few preprinted paper warning
signs reading DANGER: TOXIC CHEMICAL
SPILL and STREAM CLOSED DUE TO
BACTERIAL CONTAMINATION; a package

of waterproof firecrackers; a tube of fast-acting but easily removable Warden Baffler wicker glue to temporarily cement shut an incriminating creel; a microscopic matchbook to place next to a fish prior to taking a picture; and a tape measure with modified Fibonacci-series inch markings that read 1"–2"–3"–5"–8"–13"–21" . . .

vest

waders One-piece, hip- or chest-high waterproof footgear which both at the time of purchase and during subsequent use is guaranteed to give an angler a soaking.

waders

wading

The most common means through which a dry-fly-fisherman is transformed into a wet-fly-fisherman.

wading staff

Although specially designed collapsible metal poles are available to help anglers keep their balance as they pick their way over slippery rocks, many fishermen prefer to use an old golf club shaft, a ski pole, or the handle of a hoe, all of which not only serve as cheap and reliable substitutes, but also provide a useful reminder of the constant availability of alternate pastimes.

wahoo

1. Saltwater game fish similar to Spanish mackerel. *2.* Remark made by angler who inadvertently sits on a treble-hooked saltwater fishing lure.

wahoo

walleye
1. Large, flavorful member of the perch family with great sport value that generally feeds during low-light conditions in the evening and night hours. *2.* Discoloration of the skin around the eye suffered by walleye fishermen returning to a cabin in the dark.

waterproof

Term found on garments indicating that they are capable of repelling exterior moisture for 181 or 366 days, depending on the nature of the warranty.

whale Giant marine mammal nearly eradicated by overfishing, now hunted by practically no one except the Japanese, who claim to take the leviathans solely for research purposes, like trying to figure out how to balance a quarter-ton piece of whale sushi on a 40-foot ball of rice.

X Symbol denoting the thickness of a leader, or the gauge of a wire hook, or the strength of an angler's language when a fish escapes after the leader parts or the hook breaks off.

ZZZZZZZ

1. Sound made by patient angler waiting for a bite.

2. Sound made by insect about to deliver one.